MOON DANCE

ALSO BY SUSAN DEBORAH KING

Poetry:

Tabernacle: Poems of an Island
Coven
One-Breasted Woman
Bog Orchids
Dropping into the Flower
One Life, One Meeting (chapbook)

Edited:

Fresh Testaments (anthology celebrating the 10th
anniversary of the Literary Witnesses Reading Series)
*Out of the Depths, Poetry of Poverty: Courage and
Resilience* (anthology)

MOON DANCE

Island Poems

Susan Deborah King

Antrim House
Simsbury, Connecticut

Library of Congress Control Number: 2020935314

ISBN: 978-1-943826-67-4

First Edition, 2020

Printed & bound by Ingram Content Group

Book design by Rennie McQuilkin

Front cover photograph by Chris White

Author photograph by Jim Gertmenian

Antrim House
860.217.0023
AntrimHouseBooks@gmail.com
www.AntrimHouseBooks.com
400 Seabury Dr., #5196, Bloomfield, CT 06002

In loving memory VDM and JBS

ACKNOWLEDGMENTS

Grateful acknowledgment to the editors of the following publication in which two poems in this collection first appeared:

The Island Reader (published by the Maine Seacoast Mission for publishing): "Island Cemetery," "Moon Dance"

Deep thanks to the residents of Great Cranberry Island, Maine and to the island itself for being the truest home I have ever known, for being a refuge, a community, a place to belong. For the friendships and the conflicts, the beauty and the heartbreak, all of which allowed and inspired me to grow and create. This book is an attempt to bear witness to and celebrate the richness of this beautiful, complicated place.

Sincere thanks to Rennie McQuilkin for so gracefully and graciously ferrying my manuscript into book form.

TABLE OF CONTENTS

ISLAND

Wave of sorrow,
Do not drown me now:

I see the island
Still ahead somehow.

I see the island
And its sands are fair:

Wave of sorrow,
Take me there.

Langston Hughes

MOON DANCE

CRANBERRY HAIKU

I

The setting harvest moon
spills gold milk on the Western Way.
Lap it up!

II

Drought turns grass to straw,
Lilac leaves turn down,
Overwatered blooms droop.

III

At last! Mauve summer's-end phlox heads
bud up to bloom: Chomp!
Stealth-of-night deer.

IV

The gale keened all night
like mothers of slain children.
At dawn, still fog.

V

At the cove, grateful spadefuls
over her ashes. Gulls,
a mink, two loons.

VI

So many houses now bereft
of the friends who owned them.
I hate death!

VII

Unexpected at harbor's edge:
great blue heron. We stop
and salute.

VIII

So glad, out from behind
clouds, sun lashes water
into naught but light.

I.

ACADIA FROM GREAT CRANBERRY ISLAND

I have stood before the writ-large altarpiece
of this view and watched at dawn and dusk
the sun sear its edges pink, watched
in a swound clouds moving over it,
casting shadows upon it, as if
to bless each summit and cleft.

I have come under the spell of these waters.
Their perpetual mesmeric motion
rocks me, rocks me. When wind
shatters the surface into a zillion-piece mosaic
I'm overtaken by gooseflesh waves.

Whenever a veil of fog pulls away
with wisps lingering between islands
or at peaks, again it's world's first day.
And Schoodic, its farther shore, beckons.

This beauty has so schooled me in awe,
I gasp at the merest blossom, a fly's wing,
lichen patterns, sparrow feathers –
before anything naturally fashioned,
I bow, I bend my knee.

I have traced against the sky
the outline of these mountains,
the mark an arrhythmic heart
might make upon time, the whole
up-and-down course of a life,
the scrawl of Earth's signature,
written deep inside me –
a long indecipherable name.

WEATHER

It's the great leveler.
It's what we're all under.
The suit and the hipster,
matron and maid, whatever
race or persuasion, whatever
creed or level of need, we'll
all, if we're out in it,
get drenched in a deluge.
Whatever treasures we've laid up,
whatever medals we've collected
will neither reroute the twister
nor deter the Category 5
from sweeping our houses out to sea.
Our habits, our greed for speed
have had an effect, ramping up
storms, whipping to hurricane force
a draft, and we can track it.
We can sort of predict it, but
we can't make it heed us.
We can't will a blizzard to stop at 2 feet.
Who of us, if you please, would know
how to produce azure or halcyon?
And who knows how we'll relate
to each other as it changes?
But now, still, it's the ultimate opening line,
a slip knot that binds us, briefly at least.
A word might never otherwise pass
between us and a store clerk, between
us on the ferry and a day-tripping stranger,
but one day, we agree, both sweating,

how bloody hot it is outside, and another,
basking together in the stern,
how sublime the breeze.

AWAKE AT DAWN

for Kathleen Glaser

Instead of languishing in bed,
4:30 of a summer morning, I rose
to catch the breaking of day.
Disheartening was the scrim
of bluish-gray clouds in the east.
Still, it was so wondrously early –
on the waterfront, no one else to be seen.
And, oh, the ferment of birdsong.
I looked up to greet a gull and tracked
its circular flight around the harbor.
Suddenly, there it was: the sun popped up
despite the cloud, over the lip of the earth.
How fast we are always turning!
That fluorescent orange-pink globe
laid across the water, a quivering gimlet of like color
pointing this moment straight at me.

BREEZE

Today – just today – my soles bare
to sun-warmed porch boards
amid cricket calls and the motors of boats,
a one-engine plane, I offer
no resistance to the wind.
I let it stroke my arms and cheeks.
I let it flutter my skirt and tousle my curls
and carry off the worry, I can no longer,
anyway, entertain. May the weight of it,
under this influence fan out, as have,
right now, the clouds – feathers
a giant spirit bird let fall
on its way into or out of the blue.

EVERY DAY

The shadow of a raven passes over my garden.
A white bearded man walks by with his black dog.
Fishermen brave the waves, their skin red as their catch cooked.

The news is grimmer and more unbelievable.
I take pills that keep my demise briefly at bay.
Is he looking for his lost mind, or has he given up?

The world is closer and closer to some kind of holocaust.
I am surrounded by a chorus of birdsong.
Knotweed can never be gotten rid of.

Caught in intractable complexes, many struggle to free themselves.
Buds stretch hopefully toward the sun.
No matter what, the dishes, the laundry, the cleaning all have to be done.

How can I relax with the clock ticking so loudly toward doom.
I pray to I'm-not-sure-whom for the health and safety of my children.
Why doesn't a tsunami of outrage flood the halls of government?

Insects eat to tatters the leaves of my hollyhocks.
I kiss the brow of my beloved with gratitude.
Someone innocent awaits execution.

I look forward to a breakfast of coffee, berries and granola.
An act of violence is forming in the mind of someone who feels wronged.
I wonder if the spell of a deadly pattern can ever really be broken.

A child's legs are blown off in a bombing.
The Javen rhinoceros comes closer to extinction.
I take a shower, brush my teeth and pluck my eyebrows.

I am aroused by his beard, wind on my skin, the shapes of fruit.
I lose and can't find an earring, a sock, a memory, a god.
I have been blessed by long friendships with excellent women.

In general, those who work hardest are paid least.
I question whether the worth of an individual can be measured.
I stroke the cheeks on pictures of my grandchildren.

Many who suffer are turned away for lack of insurance.
I buy a dress I don't need to console myself.
I try to imagine greeting my end with acceptance.

Women are still belittled, undervalued, bullied, raped and killed.
I abominate the rabid hatred now abroad and do not understand it.
I keep trying, but slam into bafflement.

I've uttered more expletives in the past year than in all those before.
How can I keep from being consumed by the evil in myself?
The dinner plate dahlia beams its purple at the news.

The song sparrow sings his heart out on my garden fence post.
I pray for entrée into an as-yet-undiscovered dimension
and struggle to digest the rough fare of paradox.

NEXT DOOR

in loving memory, Eugene Vance

The house is blank, over days, stays mute.
It's white face, a rebuke.
No light in the windows after dark.
The yard is bare.
I look over expecting to see his bike,
yellow with a milk crate carrier tied behind the seat,
the yard set up for croquet,
the wheelbarrow loaded with sails.
Just last year he had a new septic dug.
How can it be he'll never see how well
the gash in the grass has healed?
The plane crashed, the one he flew himself.
My hands go to my face saying no
to those last moments.
Tall and lean, his head always thrust
ahead of the rest of him,
he was curious about us, beyond
being captivated by our lissome daughters.
He drifted over, photographed our porch flowers.
Couldn't we trim the spirea to show more of the door?
He read my lines and understood, read again
appreciating things in them I never saw.
Anytime, use his dryer. *Prune* whatever
branch of his would give our garden more light.
Deeply touched by the gift of a bouquet.
Abject apologies for wanting to borrow butter.
Lastly, placed by our door, what most
would reserve wholly for themselves: a bagful of
rare and prized, hand-picked chantarelles.

EVERYDAY WONDERS: OASES FOR A GRIEF

Will the rain never stop? Day after day
tears drip and drip and drip off the roof.

First up, first to flower, chives.
Before they can emerge, the bristly purple
blossoms have to split a translucent lavender caul.

Streamers of fog are lain along a stretch of coast
as if to cordon it off, to mark its deep green trees,
its tawny rock for special notice.

The earthworm's naked glistening length
noses its long journey across the road accordion-wise,
front rings stretch apart, then press together,
back ones a beat later, pulsating forward.

At dusk the blossoming apple is alive
with subtle movement, a flock of cedar waxwings
rummaging through the fluff, nipping bugs.
Like pale yellow flames, their breasts, licking
through the branches.

A single seed, floss spider
floats on its filaments toward indeterminate ground
in which to push down its root and spread wide its leaves.

for Dorothy Silvers

APPLE BLOSSOM

after A. E. Housman

Apple trees surround me on this island.
Now, the last day of May, I'm in
an apple blossom cloud.
The branches are thick with it,
gravid with pink-tinged white.
It feels as if the flowers blush
with arousal, opening to the bee.
They're lush with brevity,
as the tree will be so soon green.
If from their hoary, belichened trunks,
knobby joints comes this
fleecy gush, these clusters
of rosy clotted cream,
then maybe with so little room,
at almost three score years and ten,
I too can still give forth.
The petals – I nuzzle them.

WHEN LILACS LAST IN MY DOORYARD BLOOMED, A BETTER MAN WAS PRESIDENT

After withdrawal from the Paris Accords

It's lilac time, early June, on this island,
my favorite point of the year. Now,
at their peak, from their lavender-pink pannicles,
with some darker, as-yet-unbloomed buds,
the breeze wafts a swoon-inducing perfume.
It's rapturous too with the brand-new green
of the leaves shimmering in the sun,
but this year, from them in shame I recoil.
I cringe and forswear indulging, as I always have,
in enjoying them, when our nation
is so unwilling to protect such beauty.
O, it is a hard and unparalleled moment
for those of us, who, until now, no matter
the degree of grief, could always take refuge
in nature and find solace. Now, the grief
is for nature itself, and we are riddled
with self-reproach for ways we have been
complicit in its destruction, for how we
have misunderstood that nature is not, as some
of our myths command and condone, for our use
but for its own inscrutable purpose, and reverence
our only honorable posture. Hence, I draw away
from these blossoms, for how much longer will they
be able to flourish in the way we have known them?
And where might we then repair for consolation?

DANCE

Encumbered by abundance,
the locust next door, hung now
with clusters of white blossom,
drooping racemes, lumbers
clumsily in place. It flails;
it galumphs in end-of-storm
gusts, which, as they keep coming,
set up an ungainly syncopation
I start to get with, lurching
and swaying, arms haphazardly
outflung, expanding
my definition of grace.

JUNE BUGS

Alone in the house, I'm afraid
someone is trying to break in.
Someone is. They bump. They bang,
hurling their fat, hairy bodies,
of rust-colored plates
against the panes
to get at the light.
It's futile. They fail.
They keep doing it every night.
I copy that.   Desperate
to get to a new stage – to escape –
to seek what we think we need –
against whatever stands athwart,
we bump. We bang.
I wonder if they have contusions too.

BLACK IRISES

They grow for her in dark profusion,
the standards dripping like hot, purple tar,
the rhizomes a gift from her former mother-in-law.
They hide the fence where her geese are penned,
noisy, fearsome fowls. Why does she
shriek at her docile dogs?
When she moved back, after her parents' death,
from all over the world, she stripped
and refinished every last stick
in the house, reroofed, re-sided it herself
and secured a part-time postmistress job.
She makes colorful, useful mats from her brother's
old lobstering lines, sells them, her handknits
and homegrowns by the side of the road.
She's been known to block a neighbor's ancient
right-of-way across her land – always mowed
weedless and smooth as a pelt – as it used to be
the path she took as a girl to the shore.
There's a live-in younger man.
In her grandchildren, she delights.
Tall, slender, blond-gone-white,
at island events, she sports a gauzy tiered skirt
and tucks behind her ear a rose.
Though in her yard she erected
a lighthouse replica studded with
seaglass and pottery shards (it's turned on
in fog), years now, she's neglected
to put in steps to her front door.

TRUCK

The sides of it are teal, mottled
with patches of rust, as if crafted, burnished
and imbued with the gravitas of Roman glass.
The owner, with no visible means of support,
his traps piled undeployed, a yellow
barricade by the side of his house –
once dilapidated, now quasi-restored –
sails by, engine purring, his chin
lifted, cigarette lit and held between
the thumb and index of his left hand,
elbow crooked out the window.
His several reported ailments
appear to be to him of no concern
when he rides down the island
of his birth as if he and this road
will never come to an end.

II

HUZZAH

I know it's only the moon's reflection,
this new, fat-with-possibility moon,
but tonight it seems the sea is dancing,
is shivering with delight at shining,
at shining itself, the waters beneath
excited to gooseflesh with light
or giving a kind of visual applause.
But maybe it's the other way round,
the moon blowing down a luminant kiss,
an appreciative smooch for the way
the waves move and keep moving,
their fetching sinuousness. And I,
standing damp in the hot August evening,
a sort of voyeur, feel my blood surge.

THE PEONIES

I have wanted to live
as they do, when, in July,
after being tucked up tight,
they fling themselves
gangbusters wide, all
their many petals
peeled to expose centermost gold,
the under ones dropping down
to receive the breeze
letting it make them tremble.
To be borne up by v's of green,
leaves cheering them full open,
day torches, blood-dark
burning with time.
To, momentarily at least,
brighten the faces of passersby
who might be shouldering
unimaginable cumber,
to strike distress with magenta fire.

CLIMBING ROSE

for Tracy Weibel

It would not thrive
as she declined,
unable to come any more
to her island home. Only
one skinny, crooked limb
meagerly blooming.
But, thanks to a granddaughter
determined to save it,
cutting it down to a nubbin,
it surged
the summer after her death,
thick with damask blossoms
and reaching to all corners
of its wire trellis. Was it her spirit,
finally unencumbered, returning,
her blood up through the vines
running to pink, gracing
the house's face, those mustard-colored
clapboards, as hers so often was,
with a smile, wry,
bemused, and – accepting
of every blessed soul who passed?

QUICKWEED

Galinsoga Quadririata

How well named! No sooner
have I pulled up a raft of them
than, literally the next day,
they are legion, which befits
their alias: *gallant soldiers.*
Storm troopers, they gang up
on my sweet pea seedlings
to arrest them or, like
party crashers they insinuate
their hairy-leaved selves,
pretending their puny, daisy-like
flowers could mingle seamlessly
with zinnias and snapdragons,
as if they don't proliferate
like cancer cells and suck
vital nutrients away from
those glamourous blossoms.
Thus, I labor on . . . seemingly
to no avail. Just as I think I've
tossed the last ones on the weed pile –
I discover another infiltration!
Scores more I missed hiding under
the leaves of squash and tomatoes.
Against the forces of destruction,
how could I ever think I'd prevail?
They're just the advance troops, vanguard
of the conquering General himself.

HOSE

I know, I know what you'll think
if I write a paean to a hose,
and, yes, well, there's
something of that about it,
of course. Wielding it does
give me a sense of projectile power
I don't otherwise possess,
especially when
I've dug a hole
and put the nozzle on "jet".
As I bore deeper into soft earth
to make way for beauty and growth,
I wonder, *Is this how sex feels to men?*
No, I'm not above those thoughts;
in fact, I subscribe to them.
But there's more.
It's the snake-like way
it moves, wriggling through grass,
as I pull it around the house
from the spigot to reach
the front flowers
and flip it, unkink it,
how it writes a green-on-green
cursive of loops and spirals across the lawn
in praise of all things botanical,
as I cast it aside
to tend to weeding and deadheading.
How I can bliss out
showering the bee balm and yarrow.
Watering's a chore I rarely resist,

and the hose is so much more
than a tool –
a sort of companion
and conduit through which
passes, at my behest,
the element to life most essential.
Diana had her hounds,
Athena her owl. The hose
has got to be a modern iteration
of Demeter's water-filled amphorae.
With it, I'm a bride of fertility
trailing a skinny green train.

ACCOMPANIST

It gets hot out here.
Weeds crop up full-blown,
seemingly overnight,
hiding and twining, and
watering in this drought
is a constant chore.
The song sparrow takes up his post –
a literal one at the garden's corner
and sings his various tune.
I always thank him for coming.
Good company, this plain brown bird
with a black mark at the center
of his streaked, pale gray breast.
Or lonely perhaps?
Does he seek me out,
amused by my efforts,
futile as they are.
Everything will be limp and
withered in a matter of days.
But in the span we have,
I hear him say, why not
foster a feast, a riot of color?
I like to call him friend,
but our sort does not have
a stellar record where
his is concerned.
If I get too close, he decamps
to a nearby branch.
Nevertheless, from this remove,
pointed in my direction,

he continues to sing,
cheering me on,
lightening my task.

BOUQUETS

Why do I labor to grow
over 20 species just for cutting
and fuss so over the arranging,
making sure salvian blue
punctuates calendula's yellow
or dahlia's purple reigns
over subjects of zinnia red
and marigold orange, playing
assiduously too with monochromes
of white and pink – for quickly
most will fade or droop?

Why do I give so many away,
gathering a summer's day
as if it could be kept,
as if these offerings could
reduce pain, restore health,
their vibrant colors thrust
at the face of death, saying
to those I care for, *Stay, stay!*
Feast your eyes on us
and bust this all-we've-got
moment wide as the heavens.

SPINNERS

for Gail Grandgent

They came to our island
to demonstrate their craft.
They set up on a porch
where we could sit and watch.
How quickly our heart rates dropped,
our muscles relaxed. Unlike us,
hurried they weren't.
Their feet, bare on the treadles,
made the wheels go.
How deftly they fed the fleece,
still lanolin tinged,
to the flyer from clouds of it
on their laps: cream, ashen, pitch,
and a hank of roving
dyed pale grey-green.
Through their fingers fibers
wound onto spindles into yarn.
They gave us the sense
we could take our stuff,
take it in our hands, crude
as it is: our loves, our dreams,
our hates, our mistakes
and twirl them into thread.
Death comes round to life,
and life again to death so fast.
If we sit at the hub,
at the center of the turning,
circling world, if we're patient
as hands of a clock,

we learned from their whirring,
perhaps we too, as spiders do
from their spinnerets, their guts,
can come up with what it takes
to make it through.

"THERE'S A SWEET, SWEET SPIRIT. . ."

for Ashley Bryan

In his late eighties and he insists
after a visit on walking me
the almost mile to the dock
to see me off. Waiting
for the ferry I take a misstep
and one of my legs plunges
between two floats.
Pain! Shock!
When someone else asks
if I want to get up,
I say, *No. I just want to stay down*
till I feel stable enough
to get to my feet.
So he, nimble as a man
decades younger, gets down
and stretches out next to me,
about a foot away.
I forget what we talked about,
but soon we were laughing.
Soon, I was up and on my way,
with a big ugly purple bruise
and a large bump on my thigh
that has never completely disappeared.
He knew he couldn't take away the pain,
but he got down where I was.
He got down where I was
and stayed by my side
till I could stand again.

SWAMP CANDLES

See
what the ditch
lifts up: petals, tiny
yellow blades massed
as a standard brighter
in July even than the sun.
Learn what can emerge
from gouges and muck, for,
only from being in trenches
will they come. Hold
your bare stalk up
to this shining
and watch it
jump!

HERO

for Michael J. Westphal
with love, admiration, and gratitude

Anything I could say would probably
embarrass him or make him wince,
but aren't we bound to pay tribute to
those before whom we stand in awe?
Up to and beyond when he contracted
early-onset Parkinson's, the excellence
of his building has been worthy of highest praise.
Several substantial homes on our island
and solid, seamless additions are testaments
to the fineness of his craft. For more than 30 years,
he has seen to the care of our home: installing
and removing storm windows and doors, turning
the water off and on, rebuilding the deck, adding
a skylight, patching immediately when roof tiles
blow off, repairing leaks, expanding the footprint,
so it looks as if the new space had always been there.
For 30 or 40 other homes, he does this too and more.

The damned scourge keeps him flailing
almost non-stop, widely, wildly. How does
he endure it? Keeps working. One Sunday
our septic backed up. He was over in a flash
and knew just where to dig to find the tank's cap
and jigger the pump till our plumber could get to it.
He has wit, always razzing me about my purple luggage
and the amount of it piled on the dock when I arrive
for the summer. Then, unasked, he loads it all onto his trailer
and takes it up to my house. When my three-year-old

granddaughter watched him for a bit and wondered,
Are you always dancing? he retorted, *Yes! I can't stop.*
Didn't you know? I'm the jazz man!

Also, he runs. Every afternoon around 4,
I see him go past our house up and down the island,
training for marathons, in which, on a regular basis,
he places at or near the top for any age group.
For a constitutionally private guy, his courage
is on public view, his runs raising funds
for the foundation started by MJ Fox.
Within his family there are other challenges as well.
Heart, grit, honor, talent, skill, dignity, kindness,
decency, class: he shows how much farther beyond
what we think are our limits we might go.

NAOMI AND THE VILLAGE

Hip cracked from a fall,
eyes too dim now to read the music
through which she breathed,
heart compromised, she,
who once was often down to the store
to hear and comment on the news,
once a gadfly buzzing over all
that wasn't right and should be,
taking "feisty" to a rarely-reached degree,
has set herself up in a be-pillowed chair
on her porch, resting her still-graceful
piano hands on the arms, walker and cane
within reach, one hearing aid gone missing.
It's her way to be in the flow of walkers,
joggers, bikers, cars, golf carts, trucks.
Sometimes, she'll slump over napping.
More often though, there's
someone delivering food or flowers,
reading her the news, which appalls her
mightily, reading her poems of an old
famous friend, or simply chatting.
She asks, *What's going on with you?*
then bends over to listen, her eyes,
more often than they used to be,
soft with interest and understanding.
She and I fulminate together about how
pain and death, now afflicting,
affecting those we love, got
put into place anyway. The plan was
wrong. Because she hasn't withdrawn,
doesn't hide, we get to keep her with us
longer than we might.

HE WHO LISTENS

for David McShea

For him the components of music are everywhere:
weedwhacker's buzz, scrapes over grating,
the dropping of rain, fingers tapping on tables,
coughs, nose blowing, the swish of clothes
going on, truck engines revving.
He mixes these, slowing or speeding them,
varying the volume with sounds he synthesizes:
song, chant, keyboard notes, percussion.
The mélange is a paean to what
we usually screen out, intensified
to the pitch of outcry.
We won't have lived until
we really hear the sounds around us,
not just what's been labeled melody.
He was labeled himself – as
somehow impaired – and in ways,
navigating the world's been hard.
But when I listen to his sound collage,
I sense how much I've missed,
how much I dismiss, for which I'm sad
and mortified, while given back
to my world, now alert, for instance,
to the susurration on yellow paper
of this pen's nib.

HER PASSING

in loving memory, Charlene Allen

The moon, just rising, no longer full,
bowed its orange head, and the wind
stopped fondling the tree tops
as the ambulance/hearse, passing
the houses of those who'd gathered
earlier by her bed, bore her body to the dock.
Her going sent a tremor down the dark.

Spunky, blond, of unbuttoned lip
and sapphire eyes, she made, without a lesson,
paintings of her island, lush and vibrant.
In a voice that burbled and was breathful,
like short laps of wave over stones, she told
at the museum the island's stories
to the visiting world. Always the last
to leave a party and the life of it,
she danced straight through her 70's like a flame.
The stars were so sharp, they gashed
the languid summer water with her name.

BLACK MOTH

How did it get in?
A little too big for comfort,
the size of a fearsome stranger's
black moustache,
it flaps around my study,
in my lamp, then makes for me
in my chair. I screech
and jump up.
It's landed on the chair back.
How closely do I want to look?
It's deeply, lushly black,
with black antennae, feathery wings,
fuzzy head, but, god forbid,
it would give me the heebeegeebees
if it landed on my arm or neck.
Off! I'd want it OFF!
But it can't hurt me.
So what am I afraid of?
Instinct sends me straight to
the creepy things that will
feed on me after I'm dead.
But not yet! Right now,
I'm definitely quick, but
what is alive if you
can't look right at
that bug-eyed thing
that scares you till
you can see some beauty in it?

FOR CERTAIN MUSICIANS

NM, GW, LW

They roll their eyes and give me a dubious smirk
when, at the end of the service, I thank them
and say their music makes a difference that is crucial.
They counter, *There she goes again with her hyperbole.*
We're only playing NOTES! I may come to worship
burdened, worried, fearful, weary to the bone,
teeming from toxic, venial rapacities, feeling slighted,
discounted – ignored, or merely indifferent and wishing
I were somewhere else. In the net, the nest their lines
of flute, piano, oboe weave up from Handel, Telemann,
Quantz, Loeillet, I'm safe and caught. Tighter,
denser, they're mesh filtering out the psychic sludge.
Round and round they're panning the gold out of my dross.
It's a sonorous, unkinking, pain-reducing massage,
or my raw ingredients simmered to a subtle, saporific sauce.
If I put myself to it – almost impossible to resist their currents'
tug – I'm a river running myself clean. I'm a balloon,
lifting off, leaving my baggage on the earth.
There are other countries than my sometimes squalid corner.
The sky is wide. In the precincts of their signature measures,
time is suspended, expanded, dissolved. Exaggerate, I do not.

ROSA RUGOSA

Thanks to culling,
the spilt blood of deer,
once again,
way above our heads
native roses billow
along the shore,
rivaling the waves
with their magenta crests.
They could be edging on
earth's vast gown
of *peau de soie* sea,
a green/pink trim
that makes the ensemble
snazzy.
In June, how can there be
so many blooms!
Regardless of whether you
take the time, they'll envelop
you in fragrance.
A slight breeze and you're
woozy with their
perfume, dancing
adagio, appassionato
across a floor of water
in the arms of your dream.

MACKEREL

So tired from a hot day doing errands,
I can barely remain upright while
waiting for the ferry on the dock.
I stare down into harbor water,
murky green as my mind feels right now.
Suddenly, just under the surface,
a school of mackerel flashes past.
Hoping for another glimpse,
I keep looking, but they don't come back.
Not a fisher, nor much of a fish eater –
though some claim their flesh is
sweet and succulent if fried
right off the hook – I'd never
want them for dinner. But,
en masse, forming an arrow,
their sleek, silvery bodies, like strokes
of underwater moonlight, their dark,
wide open eyes, streaking by
quick as life, revive me. For that,
I'd drop my baited line.

III

OTHERWISE I'D HAVE MISSED THEM

for Peter Buchsbaum

Thank you for pointing them out, since,
anxious, because of weak knees, stepping
carefully, I'd have passed over, in these
deep woods, what might be most profound.
The wood sorrel, so low and shy
under the narrow plank walkway
over the bog, their petals pink-veined,
white, delicate, yet intense, as love
too overcome to fully express itself.
I feel I'm walking through a muted,
lucent eulogy to the unknowable.

FOR ROMANCE

Is there a greater lover than the sea?
Has it a peer for passion, for constancy?
Crashing and crashing
with pure abandon against
the flanks of the land,
making waves in me too, such waves.

I lie back on stones. Warmth
they absorbed from the sun
penetrates my core. Let those beams
and ocean's moans
pour over me. Today, even the mosquitos
can have their fill of my blood.

Above, a cloud floats,
a cast-aside night dress
taken by the wind aloft.

I wish I could be quick as the leaves
to the attentions of the breeze –
quivering at the slightest puff,
swaying in gusts, when given the rush,
writhing.

It's hard not to have a crush on bugs
who, in the face of Fall, do not
crawl away,
but sing, high-pitched,
at the top of their tiny lungs,
their dying.

It takes but a flock of cedar waxwings
to ravish me. Handsome, crested,
in their black masks and red-tipped wings,
they descend on a bush I planted
expressly to lure them into view
and pluck every last one of its black berries.
To say nothing of how their churring
can stir me.

But I am wholly undone by the flowers
whose buds enfold what their blooms disclose,
genital centers, with abandon exposed
for plunder, for more chances at beaming forth
under the sun, while petals, whose colors
streak straight through my blood,
stroke the gold of light.

TERNS

for SB and BF

Friends on a porch
looking out on the sea,
mountains beyond,
are silent. They're loath
at first to speak of what
weighs on them, what
they fear could break
them at this point.
Would the others think
them petty, boring, weak?
Terns wing back and forth
before them, their calls
irritating as unoiled hinges,
intermittent bursts of an
electric drill. But it gets
those birds what they need:
fish, space to breed and thrive.
The sea, the sky are wide
and high enough to receive
and absorb this bothering noise.
So, the friends unburden themselves,
and their worry, when heard,
diffuses into a kind of music,
screeches that bring relief
and ensure, if only for today,
survival.

ORANGE LEGS

Is there a creature more nattily got up
than a semi-palmated plover, plump
as a burgher, bustling about his business
along the strand, almost incognito
among the rocks: brown waistcoat, black
cravat, his beak band on which
could rest a set of rimless spectacles?
Only his orange legs, like red socks
with a downtown suit, or a thin wrist tattoo
peeking out from under oxford cloth
betray a decided resistance, in the making,
to consistency. Of necessity, strict
conformity gives rise to whiffs, at least,
of flagrant rebellion.

I PAINT SO THE FLOWERS WILL NOT DIE

– Frida Khalo

I will take into oblivion
delphinium as my torch,
crammed with purple supernovas,
singed heart-of-flame
electric blue. I will brandish it
in the face of death and dare
that rapscallion to create anything
remotely as beautiful.
I'll live for that moment of hesitation
when death gets that it's been trumped –
that this hand, at least, it will lose.
It will have no game but to snuff us –
how much imagination does that take? –
but their colors will abide like those
that, when I close my eyes, flash
and burst unbidden through the dark.

POPPY

Screams were heard from the neighbors' house last night.
The bank account's balance is not equal to what's due.
Where and when will the next terrorist attack be launched?

The smiles they flash to passersby belie their fury.
Improvident spending will cost the family its place.
What if my granddaughter were hit by one of the bullets?

You can never really tell what anyone else is going through.
Another fine, cut glass vase could make up for some of the pain.
Grief can freeze you, soften you, or surge unstaunched.

The spider has strung its web between our doorposts.
I never noticed, faint as marks erased, the scars on her face.
The big pink poppy, after straining long, finally bloomed.

Hang around long enough and you'll be even more confused.
If the bottom line is all that counts, what can be saved?
The river of spilled blood bears all our names downstream.

BONNIE AND NATHAN

Just shy of midnight when I flick mine off,
I see across the street their light still on.
It's a great comfort denied me when
they're gone and the house is dark.
I know the light means they're thinking,
reading, wanting to learn, that they're
concerned, curious, emailing committees
they're part of, doing good works, working
for peace in the uneasiest place on earth,
or they may be crafting from pastels, paint,
thread or wood something beautiful, useful.
We chat, we interact, trade garden strategies,
play Scrabble, borrow back and forth,
share meals and from hardest to happiest,
the facts of our lives. We care for each other
and each others' families, so I feel
protected by a kindness and decency
that cannot always in neighborhoods
be assumed, and, in a time when civilization
seems to be unraveling, consoled,
just knowing they are close, by
their quiet company through the dark.

CRANE FLY

You're aptly named, for your long,
elegantly-jointed, crane-like legs,
splayed, about the size of a child's hand
across a wall or screen. After we
tangled briefly in my shower, I flinched.
I wanted to cast you out, but couldn't budge
the window's screen. You clung to the tile,
so I just kept shampooing and let you be.
When you, or a cohort, appeared on my porch,
I grabbed a magnifier to see how you're made.
Your wings are leaded Tiffanies, translucent
maple keys, your body segmented and slim.
On either side, behind your wings, hatares,
little knobs to keep you aeronautically
balanced. What use is your mouth
since you do not bite or eat, only your larvae
aid in breaking detritus down? On your short
antennae, at regular intervals, the finest
little hairs. When I tell her about you,
my daughter says by my attentions
you must be thrilled, since you can't have
many admirers outside the entomological field.
Yet you've garnered enough notice to be
nicknamed "mosquito hawk," "gollywollop."
Creature kindred, you are given to long,
meditative pauses often on or near water.
I've developed an affection for you. For once,
not too busy, unwell or tired, when the strange
invaded – and can't it also arise from within? –
I didn't pull back and bristle then push it away, but
gave it berth, and you furnished this day with wings.

PAINTED LADY

I stopped
when you lighted
on a rock
near my feet
and stayed there
one long, holy moment,
flexing and resting
your wings, black spotted,
white and orange,
streaming behind your
beige-sheathed body
like a train out of
Christian Dior.
I've watched you
drill the incurved petals
of a dahlia
and into its dense center,
envious as you drank
through your filamentous straw
its nectar, then quickly
moved to the next
bloom and beyond.
Oh, to taste that liquor
as your tongue does!
But what a deal of work,
so you've taken a pause
from your labors,
and I too
have stopped to behold you.
To what do I owe

the honor of your presence?
I feel the urge to curtsey
and to your splendor
bend low.

MOON DANCE

for Audrey Noether

The Dow is way down.
The ship of State may well
be going under. Compassion
has become the national anathema
and on our blood, the mosquitoes
are getting plastered. Death
has the upper hand as usual
and we're bushed from doing
all we can to beat it. But
on the deck behind the Barn
after the pot luck supper,
the band strikes up.
It's the Charlene Stomp
named for an islander we lost last summer
who boogied into her eighties.
Kids, teens, their parents, oldsters
are shaking their booties on grass and gravel.
With my plastic egg full of seeds I'm
keeping time to "Lay Down Sally."
On this hot August night the fire we've lit
in the brazier is popping with sparks, so
regardless, regardless,
we're shooting our own stars.
The moon is fat with golden silver
and, melted and mellow now, we let
the soaring voice of our very own
torch singer fly us there.

ISLAND ROAD

for Jorge Fressiner

The spine of our home, it starts at the dock
and ends at a path marked *No Trespass*, which
everyone ignores, and that leads to a gold-
lichened outcrop, and an accessible-at-low-tide knob.
It goes past mansions and hovels, stacks
of lobster traps, truck hulks, past the post office,
the general store, Wimbleberry, the museum with
its café, the parsonage, the church, the library, the school,
past best-in-the-world views: sweeps of sea, Acadian mounds.
It's only a little more than 2 miles long, but ultramarathoners
have back and forthed it to a fare-the-well. Old pictures
from the year our house was built show it was
barely a path and there were none of the tall spruces –
or any other trees – that line it now. Behemoth trucks
barge on empty, lumber back on it, gears wheezing,
barge off full, foundations dug. Heedless hot rods
gun 3-wheelers four times the limit to drive
their demons out. One actually more careful one
flipped himself into a ditch last week and the whole
population smarted. All day I worry my grandchildren,
absorbed in play, their eyes on the ball, will stray
in front of an innocent car. We lost a pup that way,
no one's fault. On it, daytrippers trudge, bike or take
our long golf cart shuttle. They ogle and click away at
the quaintness, the panoramas and ask, "Where is the town?
Halfway down one side: a Black Lives Matter
banner, on the other a Confederate flag, the owner of which
crosses the road to repair the other's pickup.
One opponent of broadband install planted his cart

in the way of the trench being dug for cable.
There was shouting; there were threats, but progress
trumped them. Crisscrossing it at mealtime, neighbors
borrow ingredients: butter, garlic, lemons; deepen
friendships, stitching the seam together. At dawn,
walking her dog, mugs in hand, my friend and I
stand pajamaed in its middle for a good talk. Rain,
when it starts, freckles the surface, then slicks it
like the trail of a snail. Snakes on it get squashed
into turquoise squiggles. How we'd all like to shoot out
the streetlight to get a better view of the stars. In the fog
it glows like a gone-by dandelion, like the moon
we can't see in shroud. Today a young man from
south of the border, here for a brief sojourn, guitar
slung over his shoulder like a troubadour, reached back
to strum as he walked. The tune was faint, ethereal
and lightened, on this hot day, my weary steps
as I followed behind. It was almost as if the road
were humming to itself, recalling the traffic upon it,
the lives along it, the stories of the people and trees, the birds
and stones, the never-faraway sea, the ever-changing clouds.

BOBWHITE

He's new to our island.
We'd have remembered if he'd
been here before: his call
is distinctive, emphatic.
The dot first, then the upwards stroke
of an exclamation point.
"I'm here!" he announces,
adding, "By God!" since
he's so uncommon in these parts,
way out of range and in sharp decline.
His habitat has shrunk – open scrub –
and he's hunted.
Quails are a delicacy.
I like his style. Unafraid
to be noticed. Until it became clear
how endangered too I was, I mumbled.
I couldn't be heard.
Strange bird, quaint, lumpen,
tweedy, complete with mortarboard
and pompous as a Cambridge don
going over and over the same blasted point,
welcome and stay –
but not for too long!

I WISH I LIKED LOBSTER

It's almost a crime not to,
given where I live.
But it makes me gag!
Standing on the dock
piled high with traps,
my neighbors in the boats below
loading, stacking, coiling line,
I feel like a traitor.
I respect their work,
the monumental effort it takes:
up in cold dark, chapped hands,
aching shoulders, bait stink,
hauling and dropping, middleman's take,
upkeep, crew issues, the market,
the weather – the danger.

I love their boats' classic shape,
the cabin upraised like the head
and neck of a floating outsized sea bird,
how it often bears the captains'
loved ones' names. I love
the buoys bobbing in broad, bright
heraldic splendor out in the bay,
but I hate how lobster tastes, its
texture – like fishy sponge – how
to cook it you have to kill it
and watch it die; and when you eat it
what a mess it makes. It's a monster
you have to dismember and eviscerate.
Let's face it, a lobster looks
fearsomely weird! Whoever was first

to try it must have been starved.
And the tomalley? Green slime!
The only saving grace is the big bug's
color after it's boiled – like the sun
riding the horizon after a fisherman's
long, long day. But I have to refrain
from partaking, for what kind
of solidarity would it show if
I barfed up the catch they work so hard
to bring to table? It's a good thing
their livelihood doesn't depend on the likes of me.

ODE TO THE MOSQUITO

for Brian Cabrera

How can I praise you,
nuisance, nemesis,
wielder of a nano rapier,
breeder in stagnant ponds,
blood sucker, welt raiser,
insidious buzz,
bearer of disease?
What is there to laud?
Why are you here?
Even entomologists are stumped,
offering only that masses
of you are a delectable repast
for fish and bats.
May they gorge the more!
No, you're the great leveler:
prime ministers and public workers
flee equally your scourge.
You needle us into humility –
we can't stomp you out –
and keep us guessing *what*
in heaven your purpose might be
because we didn't make the world.

JUMPING

for Kathryn Graven

It's a matter of honor on the island, a sort of baptism,
initiation rite, to fly off the dock on a hot July day
into 50 degree water. No one, not even
young bucks, stays in long. Why
after 40 years was I suddenly ready
to take the literal plunge, to entertain something
to which I was so averse? I was the
6-year-old who held up a long line
of grousing kids at least 15 minutes,
parents and swimming instructors cajoling
from the poolside, while I summoned the courage
to jump off the very low diving board.
It was the encouragement of my neighbor
who takes the dunk almost every day with her family.
She, the fearless, passionate artist, writer, musician,
mother, friend promised it would be wildly invigorating.

So on a blustery white-capped August afternoon,
with great trepidation, I pushed off with her
from the stairs leading down to the ferry. Yes!
It was a veritable shock! The cold, astringent
to my resistance, sent a charge through me.
Something in my body's core broke loose.
By risking discomfort, I slipped, easily for once
into my own skin and, unbound, felt present as my own
very physical self. Licking a celebratory ice cream cone
on the store porch afterward, surrounded by congratulatory friends,
I enjoyed the coolish sun drying my dripping locks.
Sometimes it takes a push from someone who loves you
to leap out of a self-constructed box.

IV

JUST TIME

A day at last with no agenda
but to notice
how its stem bows,
as if in obeisance to a queen,
when the bee lands
in the geranium's cerulean cup.
How weighty is the bee
and how light
the leaves of its balm,
trembling with expectancy
at the merest current
as the hummer comes,
its back glistening with a green
of far more moment
than any tender,
drawn inextricably
to the flower's red fire.
To be the object of such desire,
to be so wildly alive,
to let death whet the blade
of experience
and have one's essence be
to another
utterly essential,
for sips of it
to keep aloft
such scintillance.
Ah . . .

WITH DOROTHY

On a walk with her in her second (maybe third-)
hand sweater with burs still attached to it
from her last foray, I see much more
than I ever would alone. She knows
a ground-hugging greenery as
Golden Thread and shows me it's
the root color gave it its name.
We pause before the "plate" of what she
remembers once to have been a magnificent,
but now blown-down yellow birch.
We gaze upon it long, its twinings more intricate
than lettering in the *Book of Kells*.

When we reach the shore, she says she loves
to come out here just to breathe. And so we do,
in silence for a while. We discuss a local
dispute for which she, unfailingly
thoughtful and sensible, suggests a simple,
practical solution that would satisfy the needs
of all involved. On the way back to the road,
we stop amid trunks of spruces that have almost
run their course. Though she doesn't approve
of the cleaning-out that's being done here
of brush and windfall, she finds the spot,
shafted now with afternoon sun, so peaceful.
She has no truck with slavish orthodoxies
and seemingly aligns with what any
given moment might require.

From the car she points out a patch of cedars
I never noticed and turns an appreciative eye

toward a bedraggled shadbush I can only see
when it's in blinding white blossom.
Then we take another path she's discovered
down to The Pool, where we hope for
a flight of plovers and get one, shifting
and shining in day's end light. With her late
beloved husband, she used to hunt in vain along
these edges for sweet grass natives once gathered
for basketmaking. Does she ever feel her husband's
presence? No, Not at all. Without such consolation,
One just somehow goes on. She suggests wetting a hank
of the grass I was once given to bring back its smell.

We mourn the passing and befrailing of dear,
older mutual friends, and she rejoices
that our knees still allow us such explorations,
remarking wryly that it won't, however, be for long.
In her company it feels as if the field of perception
is like it is in some dreams where you discover
your house has many more rooms
than in waking life you were ever aware.
Only with her it's the wider world.

GOOD COMPANY

for JET

With how many people could you sit
on a drizzly day in the middle of a field
quietly watching the slow movements
of fog, the be-spruced outlines
of the mainland veil and unveil itself
time and again like an ambivalent bride
with no breaks of sun and only a couple
of unidentifiable ducks floating off shore
for interest? How many would be glad
to do this with you for over an hour?
Few, I'd judge. But she does, my
new-found friend, with squibbits of talk,
with sighs of awe and satisfaction,
with spells of ambling along the wrackline
picking up, examining, and setting
rocks back down. Her presence
gives dimension to the moments
and creates a diaphanous
chamber for regeneration.

BLAIR

Some town officials wanted to order him
to "clean it up," but to most of us,
Blair's plot of ancient trucks and other
heavy equipment is a physical paean
to machinery. He takes hulks others
have given up on, and through his
unfathomable genius, makes them run.
So venerated, they take on a kind of
rusted patina, the aspect of gods.
He's even given some of them names
like "The Happy Executioner"
and "Fat-Bottomed Girl." With them,
despite acute, persistent back pain,
he moves earth, moves boulders, chops,
splits and chips wood, hauls and deposits,
under town contract, plows snow
from island roads, and gratis, hand-digs-out
those too old to do it themselves.
After the hurricane hit, he was the one,
at personal risk, and who knows how,
to clear paths of downed power lines.

Sturdy and square-built as a truck cab,
with piercing blue eyes, a head of hair
curly black, and possessed of a genial
temperament, he gets a kick out of
giving kids rides in his dumper.
While many other drivers won't,
driving down island, high and slow atop
his front loader, he waves. It's hard to imagine
that in his youth, he bulldozed onto its roof

the cabin in which his girlfriend was
carrying on with another bloke. This
is an island story often told with
an admiring smile. It was vacant
at the time and no one hurt.

He doesn't have a head for numbers
or words – you might not always
get a bill, or get it a year later – but for gears,
axles, cylinders, valves, pistons and shocks.
Our almost new (to us) golf cart wouldn't start.
He checked it and knew
what it needed immediately:
a solenoid (we had never before heard
of such). He fished into his supply and found
the exact one. He's become a verb: any vehicle
needs fixing – it's very expensive to barge it off –
get it *Blaired*! Without him, movement on the island,
beyond foot traffic, would grind to a halt.

THROUGH THE WINDOW

for Eileen Richards

Come to order around the kitchen table
in the Community Center, we discuss
the menu for the Harvest Supper –
biscuits, fish chowder, apple crumble –
entertain bids for fixing the leaky roof,
and, while we move and second, a mystic
element is introduced. Out the window
mist, rolling off the Atlantic, drifts
over the soccer field, detaching wisps
that float toward the road. Mixing
with sunlight, sifting it into luminous particles,
it almost looks, on this end-of-summer day,
like snow. In the little civilization we've
mustered here on our island outpost, just off
the continent's edge, we're not so caught up
with the business at hand as to be oblivious.
We pause and smile. Where else would such
a meeting be interrupted thus? To have chosen
to live where we're quick to, intimate with
natural forces, makes us proud.

RESPITE

Suspending for a moment tasks and chores,
late summer afternoon, I sit on the porch.
It's been a long stretch of stress, illness, loss
and frenetic activity. Right now I can no longer
engage with my own troubles or those of the world –
crashing markets, desperate refugees, deadly
bigotries, extinctions – which normally
I have, to a degree, some space to accommodate.
I give my full weight to the Adirondack chair
and Ottoman, the paint I laid on them myself
cool against the backs of my legs. Behind
the house clouds so white they look bleached
billow up, mimicking the mountains beneath them.
Before me the tall red maple collaborates
with breeze and sun to dapple me with shadow,
laying on me over and over the shades
of its big leaf hands. It's as if the tree were
davening over me in an effort to treat
my exhaustion. The ocean beyond it chimes in
with its sparkling incantations. And flowers,
tired from blooming, nod in approval. In this
airy chamber, attended by the elements, I hope
to be able to open again the doors to my heart.

RECIPE

How brave the flowers are!
That they break out from tiny,
suffocating cells and tunnel
through their burial to the air.
How they stretch to stems,
not knowing whither the stuff
they're made of comes from,
whether, when they reach for
substance, it will appear. Then,
they do not scruple further to emerge,
but surge, thrusting their truest colors
into the blue, their tenderest parts,
their hearts, exposing them
perforce to storm and scourge,
to drought, pillage, rot, burn
and the scissors of some, who,
besotted by their beauty,
cut them off in their prime
to clutch for private delight.
Those remaining stand nobly
in the waning light, wizening to gold,
splitting their seed pods in grief
and thanks – it's been glorious
under the sun to bloom – till,
felled betimes by frost, they're
folded into loam that would give
the next generation rise.

TIMOTHY

Because I must,
though I wish
it were different,
let me go like
these fat celadon staffs
daubing the sky
with tribute
transmuting
into numberless
tiny bright purple seeds,
clinging, quivering
that take all summer
one by one,
as they fade to mauve
and become incandescent,
for the wind
to nudge loose.

FOR COMPANY

All the houses around me now are dark.
There's no one here tonight but the moon,
a moon the shape of a seed pod about
to split its seams and let loose its bounty.
The moon and the insects singing
summer's end, summer's end to the grasses.
The moon, the insects and the surf
sobbing against the shoulders of the earth,
inconsolable.   The moon, the insects
and the surf with its infinite longing.
Oh! and the stars like gems spilled
on the dark floor of heaven with long fingers
of cloud combing through them
for the ones that take their fancy.
And the buoy bell. The buoy bell,
tolling all moments holy.

V

RAVEN

Black as incontrovertible
fact, its croak speaks to me
in death's tongue.

WITHOUT ITS CAPTAIN

in loving memory, Ev Shorey

His boat bobs and rocks on its tie-up spot,
vessel once so eager for adventure, missions
of friendship, sunset cruises down the Sound.
How he would smile in deep, shy contemplation
of the day's dying colors, facing his own end
with astonishing inborn calm.
Tall, slim, in his blue, open-collared
oxford cloth and soft-brimmed hat,
he carried himself with unstudied elegance
and took his days with a slow, balletic gait,
each step seemingly a deliberate pleasure.
Devoted, uncommonly, to his mate and kids,
he was steady in sudden fog; he was fair
and humble, kind and strong. If he could
have – and he tried with all his might –
he would have ferried the nation
through gales of its undoing to a shore
of decisions based on love, but, discerning,
also knew when not to set out at all.
For neighbors needing it, there were often
quiet envelopes of help. When you called,
he responded as if you'd just given him
the best gift in the world. If the evidence of one
decent soul is what it would take to save
all humanity, we'd nominate him.
To think of never again being helped aboard
his craft opens a cavity inside empty as his cabin.
May he have a docking smooth as those
he executed himself. His equal?
In my experience, never before,
unlikely again.

JBS

Beyond the bright colors she wore,
that she was: purple, lime green,
burnt orange, the bold stripes,
wild prints, thick bangles and big beads
on her tall, gawky, compromised –
due to age and polio – though, nevertheless,
commanding frame, her mop of chestnut
curls that even at 90 refused to gray,
the snorty laugh, the horsely voice
that spoke out fearlessly for civil rights,
women's rights, environmental protection
and that overrode protocol, insisting
on being heard, when the welfare of
family or friends was concerned
and might at a dinner table, when
conversation drifted to drivel, bark out
timely/timeless topics to discuss
(*Am I being bossy?* she'd ask
with a sly smile, then later lie awake
raking through her day's comments
hoping none were hurtful), and the way
she ate with such relish, all the while
chiding herself, afraid she'd miss something
crucial if she couldn't taste everything –
                                    beyond this
incomparable and consummate vivaciousness,
what is lost from her having to "fly away,"
as she put it, is how she might ask you
to lie next to her as she was waking
from a nap and impart, as if offering
from her deep cache of secrets, jewels

or morsels of exotic fruit, for flamboyance
and passion extended far beyond her youth,
and, calling out of the blue, how she would
probe you for your own truths to find out how
you *really* were, not those polite, packaged versions
you would use to fend off questions like hers –
What was the happiest time of your life?
I mean the very happiest?
What are you most afraid of not doing
before you die? She painted and wrote,
designed gardens and decorated houses,
collected for their appeal fine quilts and crockery,
yet disparaged her skill and wished
she could she could be a "real" artist,
though she went the eleventh mile
supporting so many others. But,
in my experience, where she truly excelled
was in wanting to *know* and creating fast
personal joinery. When she had peeled away
the husks protecting your kernel self,
since she presented her own, you could trust her,
there was such a current between you,
such a charge, the life force surging,
coursing fresh and pure in a way you
cannot now recover without her.

ANOTHER PERSON REALLY CAN MAKE A
POSITIVE DIFFERENCE IN YOUR LIFE

in loving memory Virginia Donchian Murray

Almost 90, halting and bent, she sat me down
and, from behind, put her hands gently on my shoulders
and told me to rest. She told me to rest.
Yes, I was tired, arriving later in the day than I'd said,
to see her after a cross-country car trip.
She set the *Times* and the latest *New Yorker*
at my left, and, to my right, a full glass of water.
My own mother had been too impaired
to meet many of the needs I'd had.

At her table set with colorful linens, lit candles
and a wildflower bouquet, there was always room for guests
and for discussion and debate, seasoned with prodigious laughter,
of issues large and light. Her floors were painted orange.
Hospitality was her métier. Repeated invitations to her island
led us to settle there ourselves, the place of all the many
others I've lived, most home.

Every meal for her was ceremony, if not soiree, though the fare
was simple: chicken baked with onion and carrot, reheated
leftover rice and oiled garden greens, almost always accompanied
by thin slices of just-shy-of-stale buttered, toasted bread.
For dessert, ice cream with sauce made from her own
rhubarb plants, or maybe just the sauce itself which
I could never reproduce from her recipe, characteristically vague.
She urged on us every scrap, as she could not abide waste.

Once she tended me for days when I was taken, while visiting her,
with a deadly virus. She washed my soiled clothes and sheets,
set flowers and intriguing books by the bed, and tempted me
back to health with crackers and broth. When I recovered enough

to leave, she wondered if I could stay a longer while.
Was she lonely? Well, so was I. And in her company so much less.

The first time we met I was stunned by her beauty, maintained
with no effort needed through all her years: her sepia skin and shocks
of black/white hair. She stood in her doorway, smiling a radiant and
genuine welcome unique to my husband's very large ethnic clan.
Was it because she'd suffered losses similar to mine
or because warmth was her natural response
to anyone who crossed her path?
Over time, we became closer and closer friends melting with affection
the generation gap.

When stranded together in Istanbul, she confided to me some
of the hard and glittering secrets of her earlier life, unwrapping them
slowly: heirlooms, fragile and precious.

I can't bear now
to drive through the town where she lived when not on the island.
And it feels like a travesty to confine to a page a soul
so dear and great, to put her into a type-faced coffin
and – God forbid! – bury her again. But the need
to attempt tribute is strong. She should be writ
into the view she climbed steep stairs to see out her bedroom window
against the wishes of family and friends worried for her brittle bones,
her weak back and knees. She'd send her spirit out
to the rocks and trees, to the mountains and the outer islands,
to the coast further down East, to the sky and clouds,
and to the sea, to the sea, the sea – and beyond.

DONCHIAN MURRAY (1992-2017)

No matter how much there was of it,
nor how intense, the love
we want to believe is all and conqueror
could not diminish the force
of the currents he contended against,
holding in place, the best he could manage
for moments at a stretch.
It provided only very temporary respite,
if that. In the wake of the deterioration
of his strength, of his being torn
away from us downstream,
our hearts burst with sorrow and protest
into blossoms of defeat.
We lay them on his grave as memorial
to the delight we took in him as a child,
to the flickering of his spirit's candle,
the courage and fortitude, however
tentative, he could muster,
whispering, *What more,*
what more could have been done?

DRAGON

So spent from manic caregiving
I can hardly walk,
I somehow stumble to this little cove
by the home of someone dear
no longer able to inhabit it,
just to be near her spirit.
I stretch out on the sun-warmed rocks
and feel the earth under me,
holding me up, its support.
I watch the gulls soar and sport,
dropping mussels onto a boulder
to crack them open for their dinner.
Up, back down, up and down again.
The chores we all keep doing
just to endure. I look mindlessly
up at the sky. A single oblong cloud
floats into view. It seems to sprout
wispy claws, a long, forked tongue,
a spiked, upraised tail, spines, scales.
Playful, fierce and fearsome, primal.
Energy. Regeneration. Maybe when
we finally come to rest, such images
can appear. If it did not exist somewhere
within me, would I be able to see it at all?

TREATMENT

It's a warm, breezy sunny afternoon,
so why am I inside in the living room?
Because I didn't want to miss
getting a treatment. All I have to do
is sit in the arm chair and let
the shadows of the lilac and maple outside
flecker over me. It feels like being
touchlessly massaged. The branches
and leaves dip and shimmer as if
to dispel ennui, to restore energies
or to cleanse and bless as with
the smudging of sage or the clearing
of an aura with the feathers of eagles.
The whole space is filled with their dance,
their ecstatic interaction with light.
I can't help being stirred and renewed.

THISTLE

Islesford

Except for a few dabbings
at August gold, their purple's lost,
gone flossy. Thorns at the stemtop
have softened to puffs, to buff
to be carried aloft, abroad in
a kind of botanic blitzkrieg exit strategy:
bomb the hell out of earth
so you won't have to die completely.
Float down the fairy paratroops
to colonize and multiply,
extending your time and territory.

Where flowers are, as they are here,
mostly allowed to run as they will,
a prickly thicket of this
has a corner on the field.
Could I ever let go my color,
my tips so seemingly blissfully?
A silken tuft brushes my shirt –
to caress my mortal anxiety?
Tagged, dubbed, nudged, I would
send forth words which might,
with the tiny, pointed, black-seed-like
serifs on their letters, pierce hearts
and lodge in them to flower.

ISLAND CEMETERY

Wanting to know every inch of the island,
and, till now, missing this enclave, I stumble
over hummocks that are the dust of
Stanleys, Bulgers, Spurlings, Birlems.
Many of the stones are tumbled, some
canted, all lichened, some almost completely
swallowed by the ground. Others
are face down: just their blank backs up.
The whole lot's covered in a blanket
of cranberries – not eternity's worst
accommodation, along with wind strokes,
the view and soothing voice of the sea,
upon which several here as captains sailed.

Much, mostly sorrow, can be told from numbers.
Ella Florence, her three: Clyde, Viola, Bernice,
lost long before she. Graves of unnamed
infants marked simply, 9 days or 1910-1910.
One pure, piercing exclamation: *Gone, gone,*
dear Della's gone! 19 yrs, 3 mos, 20 da.
War dead: 1918, 1944, 1953. More recently
in a corner, almost apologetically, two young, beloved
sons of summer residents, obliquely related cousins.
A wife of two buried near both her husbands,
outliving each and one of her children.

Women are designated "wives of," but men not
"husbands." One stone just says *MOTHER.*
I rail at lives reduced only to a role! What were
their thoughts, their habits their qualities?
Sayings imply death as relief from buffeted lives

of strife, danger and exhaustion: *At Rest. Gone*
Home (with an index finger pointing upward).
Drop the anchor, furl the sail. The soul is safe
in heaven. Sounds almost appealing.

How can I get in? I understand there's a steep
initiation. No one's clear who owns this plot
or from whom to ask permission. Going by the names
alone: Alma, Albion, Emery, Nellie. Wyman,
Velma, Elvira, Augustus, Amaziah, Meltiah, Arno,
Mabel, Enoch (several), Ida, Clarence, Luella
among the smattering of the Georges, Marys, Charlies,
Edwards – unusual, exotic, old-fashioned –
the company seems intriguing. There's no
surer way never again to have to leave
this place I've loved more than any other
than to be buried in it. No more tearful partings
on the dock in September. But, if they took a vote,
would these herein even consider admitting one
who plied words for a life instead of the ocean?

OF GREATER MOMENT

than ancient, obstinate enmities, celebrities, scandals, sports scores,
the S and P, the GNP, FaceBook, new looks, crimes or bottom lines,
but not, perhaps, than children harmed by gunfire, hunger, abuse,
neglect, detention, or pollution, nor the extinction of the Amur leopard,
the bleaching of The Great Barrier Reef, nor anyone made homeless
by fire, flood, cyclone, quake, tsunami, nor anyone because of
discrimination terrorized or killed, nor the approach of a world-smashing
asteroid, yet, though deemed by most unworthy of report,
nonetheless, recently of consequence

has been hearing for the first time at 2 AM a barred owl
who-whoing at the moon,
a supermoon rising, a great red pomplamous, from a sea of ultramarine,
a mink slinking his long, dark length under a neighbor's porch,
three fauns grazing, their spots luminous in fog,
a bald eagle dive-bombing right in front of me,
a great blue heron on a low-tide rock, its question mark neck
silhouetted by sunset,
a Blackburnian warbler's feathered flame hip-hopping through a maple,
every evening, the hummer zooming in for his bee balm cocktail,
a snake scrawling his black-yellow signature through my bean plants,
an eleven-foot-high multi-headed sunflower planted from seed,
a tail-end hurricane, sending the beauty bush into ecstatic spasms,
the double arc of a dolphin, as if waving his dorsal fin, right beside
the mailboat, at night, on water, all lights killed,
the heavens in heart-stopping array,
and two friends, one from the front, one behind hugging me
as I wait for biopsy results.

BIRTHDAYS, SUMMER'S END

for DR, CSR, AS, DS, JM

My life has been with you, my friends.
How many years have we together
bid the summer reluctantly adieu
with feasts and toasts and candles,
champagne and presents, and stories of our youth,
following the moon's light made wild by water
back to the island. Our children are more
than the ages now we were when we first gathered.
We have borne with one another through
their growing. Am I wrong
that it's sweeter every year we celebrate,
wondering who will be the first
to go missing from our circle?
Precious laughter. Arms around shoulders.
The tide is high now as it ever gets.

CANTICLE FOR A BURIAL AT SEA

for Audrey Noether in memory of Peter Eldredge

Beloved one, we suffer to release
your remains to these waters.
We can hope, but we don't know,
that the arms of the Mother might enfold you,
and we forbear believing we too will follow.
As we stand here on deck without you
by our side, watching the cloud of your ashes
wreathed in flowers float away
beyond us, forever beyond,
how can we withstand this unendurable
                              good-bye?
We will light in our hearts the flame
of your memory. We will tend it.
We will let it burn. We will
keep it burning. For your time among us,
Oh! the joy.

SHROUDS

Crickets and crumpled, grounded leaves
signal it's time for the ceremony
of shrouds. I shake them out: old white sheets
another beloved, now-gone islander to me
passed down, a sound somewhere between
a snap and a whomp. I drape them over the beds,
over chairs and couches to keep off the mice
and prevent further fading while our not-
winterized house waits through the cold
for our return. Every day while we're gone,
though our shades are partially drawn,
sunlight travels over our walls and art,
time turning us further and further away
from all, this summer, we've enjoyed and endured:
the bounty of flowers, the failed peas, late drought,
the gatherings, the meals with family and friends,
bonds broken, mended, strengthened,
memorials, our children's struggles, celebrations,
quiet meditations by the shore, waves washing
some of our tensions out to sea.
Somehow there's comfort in this ritual along with
sorrow. Creases hold where they've been folded,
in these effigies for the absolute end
of this season, of this chapter of our lives.

ASTERS

As if to soften the blow of oncoming cold
they crop up in clumps buffering the field edges.
Are they grounded, true to the origin
of their name, stars huddled together for warmth
or tired, bedded down clouds? As all the gold
is fading – black-eyed, rod and tansy – dusk,
summer's last color, takes over. Grief flower,
your rays, bit, supernumerous, melancholy,
are batted lashes aimed straight
at my sorry-to-be-leaving heart.

HUM

It's a mix – cicada, cricket, other locusts.
With what insistence they inveigh against
the end of flowering, their own existence!
But there is something, too, so ecstatic
about it, this protest. So sustained,
so intense. Not the relentless sirens
of my Kansas City girlhood – here in
New England, more subtle: millions
of tiny jingling bells, a wavery vibrato,
treble continuo, melding to an underpitch
for the plain song of our light-waning days
that yet drills through, unignorably,
to consciousness: *To have lived!*
Just to have lived!

ABOUT THE AUTHOR

Susan Deborah King, M. Div, has taught Creative Writing and led retreats on creativity and Spirituality at various institutions in Minnesota and New England. She is the author of five other full-length poetry collections including *Coven, One-Breasted Woman,* and *Bog Orchids.* A mother of grown twin daughters and a grandmother, she lives in Maine with her husband, Jim Gertmenian.

This book is set in Garamond Premier Pro, which had its genesis in 1988 when type-designer Robert Slimbach visited the Plantin-Moretus Museum in Antwerp, Belgium, to study its collection of Claude Garamond's metal punches and typefaces. During the mid-fifteen hundreds, Garamond—a Parisian punch-cutter—produced a refined array of book types that combined an unprecedented degree of balance and elegance, for centuries standing as the pinnacle of beauty and practicality in type-founding. Slimbach has created an entirely new interpretation based on Garamond's designs and on compatible italics cut by Robert Granjon, Garamond's contemporary.

For more concerning the work of Susan Deborah King,
visit www.antrimhousebooks.com/authors.html
This book is available at all bookstores
including Amazon.